Holy Places

The Western Wall

and other Jewish Holy Places

Mandy Ross

www.heinemann.co.uk/library
Visit our website to find out more information about **Heinemann Library** books.

To order:
 Phone 44 (0) 1865 888066

Send a fax to 44 (0) 1865 314091

Visit the Heinemann Bookshop at www.heinemann.co.uk/library to browse our catalogue and order online.

First published in Great Britain by Heinemann Library, Halley Court, Jordan Hill, Oxford OX2 8EJ, a division of Reed Educational and Professional Publishing Ltd. Heinemann is a registered trademark of Reed Educational and Professional Publishing Ltd.

OXFORD MELBOURNE AUCKLAND JOHANNESBURG BLANTYRE
GABORONE IBADAN PORTSMOUTH NH (USA) CHICAGO

© Reed Educational and Professional Publishing Ltd 2002
First published in paperback in 2003
The moral right of the proprietor has been asserted.

Designed by Joanna Sapwell and StoryBooks
Illustrations by Nick Hawken
Originated by Blenheim Colour
Printed in China by Wing King Tong

ISBN 0 431 15514 3 (hardback)   ISBN 0 431 15521 6 (paperback)
06 05 04 03 02   07 06 05 04 03
10 9 8 7 6 5 4 3 2 1   10 9 8 7 6 5 4 3 2 1

British Library Cataloguing in Publication Data
Ross, Mandy
        Western Wall – (Holy places)
        1. Jewish shrines – Juvenile literature 2. Western Wall
        (Jerusalem) – juvenile literature
        I.title
        296.4'82

Acknowledgements
The Publishers would like to thank the following for permission to reproduce photographs: AKG Photo pp. 6, 9; Associated Press p. 19; Christine Osborne Pictures pp. 20, 22; Circa Photo Library pp. 17, 21; Circa Photo Library/Icorec p. 27; Corbis/Archivo Iconografico, S.A p. 11; E & E Picture Library p. 12; Getty Images p. 28; Link Picture Library pp. 7, 10, 24; Photodisc p. 25; Popperfoto/Reuters p. 18; Powerstock Zefa p. 26; Robert Harding Picture Library p. 8; Trip/A Tovy pp. 13, 14, 16; Trip/H Isachar pp. 15, 29; Trip/H Rogers p. 23; Trip/R Seale p. 5.

Cover photograph reproduced with permission of Ords Eliason\Link.

Our thanks to Jon Mayled for his assistance in the preparation of this book.

Every effort has been made to contact copyright holders of any material reproduced in this book. Any omissions will be rectified in subsequent printings if notice is given to the Publishers.

Contents

Words printed in bold letters, **like this**, are explained in the Glossary on page 30.

What is the Western Wall?

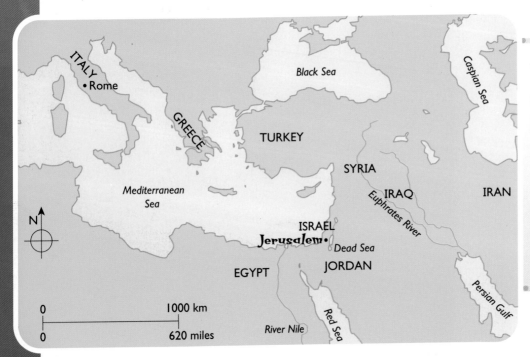

This map shows Israel and the countries of the Middle East

The Western Wall is a holy place for Jews. It is in Jerusalem, a city in the modern-day country of Israel. Today, Jews from all over the world go to **pray** at the Western Wall. Many pray for peace, in a land that has seen many wars.

The Western Wall is all that is left of a great Jewish **Temple** in Jerusalem. The first Temple was built about 3000 years ago, by the Jewish king, Solomon. For over a thousand years, the Temple was the place where Jews went to **worship**. Twice it was attacked and pulled down, but each time it was rebuilt. The Western Wall was one of the outer walls of the last Temple.

What is Judaism?

Judaism is the religion of the Jewish people. It is an ancient religion. Jewish people pray to one God, just as they did 4000 years ago. They pray at the **synagogue**, and read from their holy book, the **Hebrew Bible**. The **Torah scrolls** contain part of this Bible.

After it had been built for the third time the Temple was destroyed at last in 70 CE by the Romans. It was never rebuilt. There is no Jewish Temple today.

Jerusalem is a **holy** city for three **religions**: Judaism, **Christianity** and **Islam**. People of these religions have lived peacefully side-by-side there. But there have been many wars over Jerusalem. There is still fighting there today.

The Western Wall. It formed part of the courtyard of the last Temple.

Why is the Western Wall there?

Abraham was one of the first Jews. He lived over 4000 years ago, in the dry desert land of the **Middle East**. At that time, the city of Jerusalem was not yet built.

The **Hebrew Bible** tells how God called Abraham to a rocky mountain called Mount Moriah. There, God told Abraham to **sacrifice** his beloved son, Isaac. Abraham found it very difficult and thought it cruel, but because he loved and respected God he wanted to obey. At the very last moment, God told Abraham to stop, and to sacrifice a ram instead. Abraham had proved his love of God, and Isaac was safe.

This painting shows an angel stopping Abraham from sacrificing his son Isaac

Desert mountains like the land around Jerusalem

The city of Jerusalem grew up around Mount Moriah. Hundreds of years later, Solomon built his **Temple** on the spot where Jews believe God spoke to Abraham.

DID YOU KNOW?

The three religions of Judaism, **Christianity** and **Islam** believe in one God. The story of Abraham is also told in the **Muslim** holy book, the Qur'an. In the Qur'an Abraham is called Ibrahim. The Qur'an also says that God asked Ibrahim to sacrifice Isma'il, his other son, rather than Isaac.

Solomon's Temple

A model showing King Solomon's Temple in ancient Jerusalem

In around 950 BCE, King Solomon built the first **Temple**. It was a huge and beautiful stone building, lined inside with fine wood. Every day before dawn, priests led a torch-lit procession to the Temple, ready for the morning **prayers**. The priests wore blue, purple and scarlet robes. They were decorated with tiny golden bells and gold thread.

Inside the Temple was an ever-burning oil lamp called the Ner Tamid. It was a **symbol** of God's loving presence. In the most important part of the Temple stood the **Ark**, a special chest that held the Jews' **holy** books and writings.

How do we know?

The **Hebrew Bible** describes Solomon's Temple, how it was built and what went on inside it. A Jewish **historian** called Josephus also wrote a description of the last Temple.

In 587 BCE, Solomon's Temple was destroyed by enemies of the Jewish people. Fifty years later a new Temple was built, but it too was destroyed.

The Western Wall was part of the outer wall of the third Temple. It formed a great courtyard, where children went to school, and traders gathered to do business. This last Jewish Temple was finally destroyed in 70 CE by the Romans.

This Roman carving shows soldiers destroying the Jewish Temple and taking away the holy goods

Jerusalem through history

A medieval Christian mosaic showing the walled city of Jerusalem

Jerusalem is important to **Christians**, **Muslims** and Jews. Christians believe that Jesus Christ, their leader, died there on the cross and rose again from the dead to go to heaven.

For Muslims, too, Jerusalem is a holy place. Muslims believe that the **prophet** Muhammad (**pbuh**) travelled there. He made a miraculous journey from a place called Makkah. They believe that he was lifted up to heaven from Mount Moriah.

People of many different **religions** have lived in and around Jerusalem. Jewish people have always lived in the area, ever since the time of Abraham. But most Jews were forced to leave, from around 70 CE onwards. Other people moved in. Their families later became the **Palestinians**.

The 'Wailing' Wall

Many Jews made a holy journey, or **pilgrimage** to the Western Wall. They cried at the destruction of the Temple, and **prayed** for a time when Jews could worship freely there in a country of their own. That is why the Western Wall is sometimes called the 'Wailing' Wall.

Over the centuries, Jerusalem has had rulers from different religions. The Romans ruled when the last Temple was destroyed in 70 CE. In the 12th and 13th centuries CE, Christian **crusaders** fought to take control. Later, Muslim Turkish rulers called the Ottomans took over.

The Ottomans ruled for hundreds of years, until the First World War (1914–18). After that, Britain took charge of the area. Britain promised both the Jewish and Arab peoples their own countries there.

A 14th-century painting of Christian crusaders in Jerusalem

The Western Wall today

The new state of Israel was formed in 1948. Israel is the only Jewish state in the world. Since 1948, there have been several wars between Israel and its neighbouring countries.

Between 1948 and 1967 Jerusalem was divided in two. Part of the city belonged to Israel's neighbour, Jordan. The Western Wall was in the part of Jerusalem ruled by Jordan. Jews were not allowed to go there to **pray**. But in 1967, after a war lasting just six days, Israel won the whole city of Jerusalem.

Jewish men praying at the Western Wall. Women pray in a separate area next to them.

The Holy of Holies

The Holy of Holies is the name for the **sacred** inner part of the Jewish **Temple**. The original position of the Holy of Holies is somewhere on Mount Moriah, buried under rocks and rubble. Some Jews will not go on Mount Moriah, because they do not want to step on the Holy of Holies by mistake.

For many centuries, the Western Wall had been hidden behind crowded houses and shops. But after 1967, the area was cleared to make a large, open space where people could gather and pray. Now the Wall is treated like a great open-air **synagogue**.

Above the Western Wall, you can see a beautiful golden dome. It is part of a **Muslim** place of **worship** called the Dome of the Rock, built on Mount Moriah. It is a reminder that Jerusalem is a holy city for people of several **religions**.

The Western Wall and the golden Dome of the Rock

What happens at the Western Wall?

Every day, Jewish people go to the Western Wall to **pray**. There are separate areas for men and women to pray.

The Wall is busiest on Friday evenings and Saturdays. This time is called Shabbat, the Jewish Sabbath. Sabbath means the day of rest and prayer. On Friday evenings, young Jewish people gather to pray and dance beside the Wall. This is a happy and festive time. Then on Saturday mornings, Shabbat services are held there, with singing and praying and reading from the **Torah scrolls.**

Dancing by the Western Wall on Shabbat

Prayers on paper

If you look closely at the Wall, you will see slips of paper folded and tucked into the cracks between the huge stones. When they visit the Wall, many Jewish people write down prayers and wishes. They slip them into the Wall, hoping that their prayers will reach God especially quickly from there.

On Mondays and Thursdays, **Bar Mitzvah** and **Bat Mitzvah** services are held at the Western Wall. When Jewish boys are 13 they can become Bar Mitzvah, and when girls are 12 or 13 they can become Bat Mitzvah. It means the boy or girl is beginning to be a grown-up. This is a very special and exciting time for the whole family. A boy who became Bar Mitzvah at the Wall tells of his memories on page 16.

Prayers written on slips of paper tucked between the stones

Bar Mitzvah at the Wall

Shimon Lev, from Birmingham, held his **Bar Mitzvah** at the Western Wall. Here he talks about his memories.

My thirteenth birthday was during the summer holidays, so we planned to go to Israel and hold my Bar Mitzvah service at the Western Wall. I was very excited. All my life, I had heard so much about Israel and Jerusalem! It was the first time I had ever been abroad, too.

I travelled to Israel by plane with my parents and my sister. Other relatives and friends from Britain joined us, as well as some cousins from Israel who I had never met before.

A Bar Mitzvah service beside the Western Wall

When we got to the Western Wall that morning, it was already very busy. Lots of other people were **praying** there.

My father led the service, and at last I was called to read from the **Torah scroll**. This was the moment I had imagined for so long. I read and sang in **Hebrew**. When I finished, everyone shook my hand and congratulated me.

After the service, I went right up to the Wall and slipped a note between the stones, with my own private prayers.

Afterwards, everyone came back to our hotel for a meal and celebrations. Every Bar Mitzvah day is special — but mine was extra-special because it was at the Wall!

A boy reading from the Torah scroll at his Bar Mitzvah service

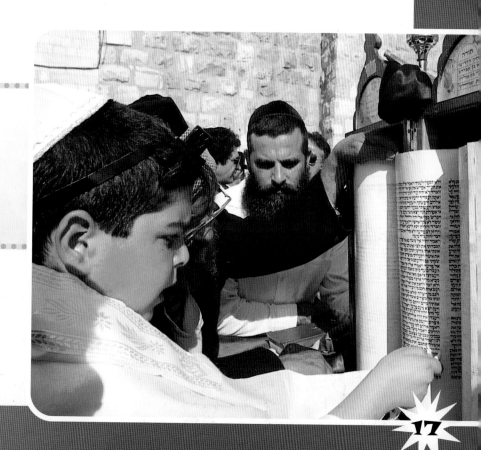

Other events at the Western Wall

The Western Wall is the religious heart of Israel. Many special services and events are held there. People gather at the Wall for **prayers** and services to remember people who have died. In 1995, the Israeli Prime Minister, Yitzhak Rabin, was killed. Huge crowds gathered for a service at the Wall to honour his memory.

The Jewish calendar is based on the Moon instead of the Sun like the Western calendar. The months have different names. Tisha B'Av, the ninth day of the Jewish month of Av, is a sad day in the calendar. Jewish people remember how Solomon's **Temple** and the other Temples built in its place were destroyed.

These people are praying and studying at the Western Wall on Tisha B'Av

Women of the Wall

Orthodox Jews are Jews who keep their religious traditions very strictly. Men and women must pray separately. In Orthodox Judaism, only men are allowed to hold and read from the **Torah scroll**. A group called Women of the Wall is calling for women to have the same rights as men to pray at the Wall. They are asking for the right to hold and read from the Torah scrolls.

On Tisha B'Av Jews also remember other terrible events that happened to Jewish communities through history, including the **Holocaust**. There are special prayers at the Western Wall on Tisha B'Av. Some Jews fast to mark this sad day. This means they go without food or drink for a whole night and day.

Men and women praying together near the Western Wall

Judaism today

Jewish people believe in one God, just as they did in the time of Solomon's **Temple**, 3000 years ago. But since the Temple was destroyed, there have been many changes. Now, instead of a temple, Jewish people **pray** at a **synagogue**. Jewish leaders are called rabbis rather than priests.

Shabbat, the Jewish Sabbath, is a special day of rest. It lasts from sunset on Friday to sunset on Saturday. On Shabbat, Jewish people go to the synagogue, and spend time at home relaxing with their families. They should not do any work during Shabbat. During synagogue services, the rabbi leads prayers and songs. There are readings in **Hebrew** from the **Torah scrolls**.

A rabbi with the Torah scrolls in a synagogue

Jewish people celebrate their religion at home, too. On Friday nights, families gather at home to light Shabbat candles and to share a meal together.

Judaism teaches people to lead a good life, and to treat people fairly. Giving to charity, and tikkun olam, which means 'mending the world', are important beliefs.

Lighting special candles at home to welcome Shabbat

What is inside a synagogue?

Nowadays, **synagogues** are used instead of the **Temple**. Jewish people go to a synagogue to meet, **pray** and learn. There are synagogues in most of the big cities around the world. Can you find out where your nearest synagogue is?

Most synagogues are built to face towards Jerusalem, where Solomon's Temple once stood. Synagogues contain things to help to remember the Temple. If you get the chance to visit a synagogue, look out for these things.

Inside a synagogue. In the centre is the Ark, where the Torah scrolls are kept.

Reading the Torah

The Torah scrolls are very important to Jewish people. They believe the scrolls should never be touched by hand. When someone is reading from the scrolls they use a special pointer shaped like a hand. This is called a Yad. This means they don't touch the scrolls.

In every synagogue an ever-burning light called the Ner Tamid shines constantly as it did in the Temple. The Ner Tamid is kept alight to remind people that God is always there.

The **Torah scrolls** are kept in the **Ark**, a special cupboard or chest. This is a reminder of the Ark in the Temple. The scrolls themselves are dressed in decorated robes, with tinkling silver bells on the top. These help people to remember the robes worn by the priests in the times of the Temple.

Torah scrolls inside the Ark

Festivals at the Temple

Many Jewish festivals celebrated today remind the Jews of the **Temple** in ancient times.

Hanukkah, the festival of lights, comes in November or December. At Hanukkah Jews remember how enemy soldiers were sent by King Antiochus of Syria to capture the Temple in the 2nd century BCE. The soldiers put up statues of their god Zeus, which made the Temple **unholy**.

A small band of Jewish fighters defeated the large enemy army. They won back the Temple. They threw out the statues of Zeus and made the Temple holy again. But they could only find one small flask of oil to burn in the everlasting lamp.

Lighting candles at Hanukkah

Pilgrimage to the Temple

In ancient times, Jews made a holy journey or **pilgrimage** to the Temple three times a year: at **Passover** in the spring, **Shavuot** in the early summer and Sukkot, the harvest festival in the autumn.

For each of these festivals, hundreds of thousands of pilgrims travelled great distances to the Temple, bringing gifts. Huge crowds gathered to join in the **prayers** and celebrations. These festivals are still celebrated today.

A painting of pilgrims visiting the Western Wall a long time ago

Jews believe that God sent a **miracle** to keep the everlasting lamp alight for eight days, until fresh supplies of oil could be fetched.

Today at Hanukkah, Jewish people light candles every night for eight days to remember the miracle.

Jewish festivals today

Rosh Hashanah is the Jewish New Year. It falls in September or October. At Rosh Hashanah there are **prayers** at the **synagogue**. The rabbi blows the shofar, a ram's horn, to welcome the New Year. At Rosh Hashanah, Jews eat apples dipped in honey as they pray for a sweet New Year.

Yom Kippur means Day of Atonement. It comes ten days after Rosh Hashanah. For a whole night and a day, Jewish people go without food and drink. They pray and ask God's forgiveness for any bad things they have done during the year.

This rabbi is blowing a shofar at the Western Wall

A Passover meal. You can see the flat, square matzah bread at the front.

Passover is a celebration of the Jews' escape from slavery in Egypt in ancient times. Today, families gather together at a Passover meal to re-tell the story.

The Jews fled so quickly from their homes they did not have time to bake their bread properly. Instead they ate very thin, flat bread baked in the hot sun as they travelled. This bread is called matzah. Jews eat matzah and other special foods to help them remember the story of Passover.

DID YOU KNOW?

At Easter **Christians** remember how Jesus went to his Passover meal, the Last Supper, before he died the next day. That is why Passover and Easter are close together in the spring. At Easter, Christians remember how Jesus died on the cross, and how he rose from the dead.

Other important Jewish places

Masada is a mountain in the desert, a few hours' drive south of Jerusalem. It is about 400 metres (1300 feet) high, with steep cliffs on all sides. It is a place that is hard to attack. The Romans had a camp at Masada, but in 66 CE Jewish fighters managed to capture it. They were fighting against the harsh rule of the Romans.

After the **Temple** was destroyed in 70 CE, many Jews fled to Masada for safety. About a thousand Jewish people made their home there on top of the mountain.

A picture looking down on the ruins of Masada

A memorial at Yad Vashem remembering Jews who were killed in the Holocaust

The Romans started to build a huge ramp up one of the mountain sides. Then they dragged up weapons to fight the Jews. It took two years to build the ramp.

At last, the Romans reached the top of the mountain. Rather than be killed or become slaves, all the Jews decided to kill themselves. In all, 960 men, women and children died. Jewish people visit Masada today to remember the people who died there for their beliefs .

Yad Vashem

Yad Vashem is a museum and a memorial in Israel. It remembers the 6 million Jewish people who were killed by Adolf Hitler and his followers during the **Holocaust**. It also remembers people of other religions, who helped Jews to survive during this terrible time. Yad Vashem is a painful place to visit. But it is important not to forget those who died.

Glossary

Ark special cupboard or chest for keeping holy books and scrolls in the Temple and in synagogues

Bar Mitzvah/Bat Mitzvah Hebrew for 'Son of the Commandment'/'Daughter of the Commandment'. Becoming Bar or Bat Mitzvah means starting to be a Jewish grown-up.

BCE stands for Before the Common Era. People can use this rather than the Christian BC, which counts up to the birth of Jesus Christ. The year numbers are not changed.

CE stands for the Common Era, instead of the Christian AD. The year numbers are not changed.

Christian someone who follows the religion of Christianity, based on the teachings of Jesus Christ

crusaders Christians from Europe who wanted to bring Jerusalem under Christian rule

Hebrew language that the first Jews spoke. Jews all around the world say prayers in Hebrew.

Hebrew Bible Jewish holy book. It is almost the same as the Christian Old Testament.

historian someone who studies the past

Holocaust the murder of Jews by Adolf Hitler and his followers during the Second World War (1939 to 1945)

holy (unholy) to do with God. (Unholy means not to do with God.)

Islam religion followed by Muslims

Middle East lands south-east of the Mediterranean Sea, including Israel, Egypt, Saudi Arabia, Iran and Iraq

miracle something that God made happen

Muslim someone who follows the religion of Islam. Muslims pray to one God, whom they call Allah.

Orthodox Orthodox Jews keep their traditions strictly without changing them

Palestinians people who are not Jewish and have been living in Israel for 2000 years

Passover Jewish festival remembering how God helped the Jews to escape from slavery

pbuh letters stand for 'peace be upon him'. Always written after Muhammad's name.

pilgrimage journey made for religious reasons

pray/prayer to think about or talk to God. A prayer is the words you think or say when you pray.

prophet someone who tells people what God wants

religions belief in God or gods

sacred another word for holy

sacrifice to give up something to God

Shavuot Jewish festival remembering how God gave the Torah to the prophet Moses

symbol sign, or something that stands for something else

synagogue where Jewish people go to meet, pray and learn

temple place of worship

Torah scrolls long rolls of parchment with the words of the Torah, part of the Hebrew Bible, on them

worship religious ceremony to show love for God

Index